Shards Of The Sun

Naman Ojha

BookLeaf Publishing

India | USA | UK

Made with ❤ on the BookLeaf Publishing Platform
www.bookleafpub.in
www.bookleafpub.com

Dedication

For my grandfather,
a believer by heart,
with whom I saw my first shooting star

Preface

This is my first book ever. It is inspired by a fraction of the life I have experienced. The sun is the center of our universe, just as you are the center of your own life. 'Shards' refers to the broken dreams, messiness, regrets, love, and everything we encounter on our journey through life. 'Shards of the Sun' represents the fragments of your existence—pieces of light and shadow that make you who you are.

To you, the readers, may this book resonate deeply. May it become something you read and then stare at the ceiling, thinking about it for the rest of the day.

Acknowledgements

I wish to thank my family and my dear friends. Every one of you is an inspiration to me. Your way of living and embracing life has always pushed me to take steps forward. If it were not for you, this book would never have come to life.

I especially want to thank my dear sister, who taught me to be carefree and to walk the paths I've always wanted to take. Your courage and love have been my guiding light. I will not say it to you but I do love you.

Thank you all for being a part of this journey.

1. The Dawn, The Beginning

A tale of undivided attention,
leading to a book of emotions.
Will I reach the finish line,
or give up as time passes by?

I might as well start,
to turn pages with my so-called art.
When I believe that I will thrive,
the universe will guide.

Maybe the book won't find anyone,
but if it does, it will pierce through hearts and time.
May it resonate with beings of every kind—
those who are lost, happy, or waiting for their time.

May they read it so loudly,
the noise of tears, chaos, and joy,
hidden within these pages,
fills the silences around and beyond them.

Lost are a billion worlds
under a single sky.
You are not the only one.

I know
you don't know where you are going,
but you will find you carried it all along, all the time.
You just have to show up,
like I carried these words,
now pouring them into the river.
They will call it a poem;
for me, they are silver linings to my way home.

If this river of words can meet the sea in the end,
trust me, on your feet you will land.
Happiness and contentment wait
on the other side.

For you, just for you,
these words were born—
like a beacon of light
in the storm.

2. Escaping in Sunshine

She dreamed—

"Oh worries, leave me alone.
I'll wander with my goggles on,
to islands wild and unknown.

Diving into oceans deep,
scaling mountains steep—
spontaneous and free.

I'll laugh as time slips by,
with friends, with wine, beneath the sky.
A joy so pure, my heart feels full,
as if time has paused, not aging at all.

Demolishing the walls that cage my soul,
unburdened by the darkness of the night—
for I am a firefly, can't you see?

Sipping coffee as the sun rises,
igniting the skies,
like a sunflower, my eyes
fill with the hope of light.

I will stand tall,
rooted deep yet reaching free—
on the muddy shores
and the mountain peaks,
writing the book of my dreams—
poems with raw emotions and broken flow,
forever straying from the point,
yet chaotically profound,
a testament to a soul set free."

3. In the sky you shine bright

I learnt to fly a kite, ma—
it touched the sky.
One day, I'll sit on that kite,
to be closer to the stars,
where you are shining bright.

These days, I'm quiet, in a fight
against the sadness and anger
that won't leave me.
Wasn't it easy to leave me behind?

But happiness won't return,
and you—you won't come back, will you, ma?

In all those years you were with me,
I lived in a world so bright.
Every day, I'd soar to a new height,
as gods poured love and affection from the sky.

Now I live in a different world,
where winters make me cry.
Once, I chased the dawn with all my might;

now I wait for the dusk and the night.

As I write, it feels as if I only had you for seconds—
not months,
not years.

So many things left unsaid.
You left this world—can you answer me now?
Would you have felt differently if I'd said those things?
Would you be happier up there?

Maybe you have forgotten me,
have taken a new form of life.
If under the same sky,
look for the kite
flying highest in the sky.

4. She, the Sunshine

I made a cup of coffee for her
and wondered if, with every sip,
the echoes of my heart would touch her soul.

She didn't know that
she's the thought in my brain.
Imagine a world inside this brain—
she would be the headlines of the newspapers,
the talk of every town, hidden in every sound.

She whispers, "Nice coffee,"
then moves on
to talk about the stupid world.
How cruel the world is
to my foolish heart.

Then,
in the pouring rain,
emotions slip by.
I wish she would turn back,
to hold me close,
see the chaos going on.

In tears I soak,
my smile long gone.

I keep writing about her,
dwelling on things
that could never be true.

Ahh—
I must take a trip to the mountains,
to go away,
maybe for some time,
away from the sunshine—
until my heart learns
she is not the sun
to my earthly soul,
but a star I once mistook for daylight.

5. Always Changing

Embracing the change,
it may seem you are just driving in another lane,
say,
with a pain that only time will take away.

Be it the cities you change,
the work you plan,
the friends—the magical elements of your life—
moving away.

This dynamic nature of life
strikes,
pinches,
but you must look forward,
for everyone is in pursuit of money and happiness.

Nothing is static,
nothing is constant.
You and I have only
limited frames of time
to share the same space,
wear the same lens.

So why hold your tears back?
Why not make another plan?
Why not breathe life together—
for now, just for now?

Break the momentum,
take a pause.
Under the stars,
driving the cars,
losing it all out,
together—because
we cannot go back,
back to the start, to the dawn.

6. Two Worlds

Two worlds collide—
He, the boundless giver,
She, the measurer, a reasoner.

Co-existing,
with questions resting in their heads:
Why is he so kind to me?
Why does she build walls for me?

In his world,
affection never poured,
love unexpressed—
Think of a book guiding his life,
its pages blank but for one line:
"You are not here to merely live,
but to impact those who depend on you."
And so,
fulfilling expectations became
his silent way of devotion.
He did look at others,
walking too fast,
thinking he would be left behind,
no matter how much he tried.

A humbled giver shaped, never to receive.

In her world,
she loved deeply,
expecting equal return,
but met with silence,
she chose to build walls,
to guard her heart wisely.
Think of a book guiding her life,
but she tore it apart and decided to write her own.
She did not just want to walk fast but to fly.

Different intentions,
creating bittersweet tensions.
He would let her know about the parts of his world;
she would listen without a hunch,
but would never tell what's new in hers.
Yet they both care deeply about each other.

If, for a moment, their sense of adventure,
music, and idea of carefree days
would often tie them together.

She is looking for a man who can build a home,
but he is a boy still learning it all.
"To build a home" and "be a home"
are different things.

In a bond of friendship they lie,
seeing each other, they smile.
This friendship is eternal-
a quiet harbor in the storms of their world.

7. Love: A moon that shines

To be loved by her
feels like a part of paradise,
whispering to fireflies,
their glow reflecting her eyes,
tenderly lit up
in the night sky.

Her smile, a burst of sunshine—
fields of flowers bloom as she walks by.
She plucks a few—
nature doesn't mind—
and she lies in the grass,
gazing up at the sky.

The wind passes by,
touching her hair,
brushing a strand across her eye.
She turns to me, says,
"With you, I feel at home—"
still, serene, and so at peace.

And on the contrary,
I feel happily chaotic,

fleeing away from the real world,
talking to the moon,
for I have found my earth,
forever reflecting the light of her love.

Oh, what a magical universe,
to be loved by her.

8. Mortals unlike the Sun

Knock, knock,
it's your life, telling you, "It's the end."
To which I replied, "But what of my regrets?"
This time, you take them with you.

In the grave, I will be hidden.
The stories I have written,
the friendships deeply woven,
the places my feet have brightened—
will I get to read them,
sing with them,
and visit them one last time?

Sunshine fading in my eyes,
my heart aches to walk, disguised,
to the people who have drifted away.
Inking letters to them,
for they have mended my days
in a thousand different ways—
with their little gifts,
little smiles and acts

Now I trace back,

all of it has turned shallow existence
into a meaningful life.
But now it is the end, oh—
hope and signs of every kind,
yet no hint of the day that we die.

In the next life,
I wish to walk the same paths,
to hold the same hands,
but this time to speak the unspoken,
to take the steps I feared,
to brightly smile in the face of defeat,
to write more, to love more,
to live a life to which I turn back and say,
"No regrets."

9. Wherever, Whenever It never dies

"What of me will you remember?
For what of me is you?"
"In the end," she said,
holding his arms.

Still,
she breathes in his story,
smiles in his days of glory.
Fragments of his existence
carry the fragrance of her essence.

He sails to tell tales
of the discovery
of the love found in poetry.

He can feel in the winds howling—
somewhere, his name, she is still calling.

Oceans afar,
or in the wars that have passed,
or when galaxies torn apart—
wherever, whenever she is born,

she will carry the fragments of the love lost,
printed in her soul.

19

10. Solar Eclipse: The sun hides

Ran out of luck,
timings now suck.
Trusting my instincts,
I had to hide emotions about you,
had to lie to you.

Decided to be lost
in translation,
where boats of truth,
ready to sail from the heart,
sink when the words come out.

On blurry nights,
I remember your face.
I imagine if you were there,
how sweet that moment would taste.

The jokes you would have made,
the sound of your voice—
every other thing would fade.
If only I could trade
with destiny,

I would bend the plans,
skip to the day
where we fell in love,
every day.

Accepting the truth
is the hardest part—
realizing you are not going to walk
into this room,
for my love is doomed.

You would not see me,
for I am just a part of the crowd.
You would not love me,
for I am that you do not think about—
a shadow in the noise,
a whisper lost in the shout.

11. Hopeful Light across the Cosmos

I dropped a wish into the well's silent depths
and stood there, still,
peering into the darkness
where hope's light should have glimmered.

I drifted into a vision:
I had won the race,
every eye turned to me,
every voice lifted in praise.

For a moment, I felt it—
the reason for my being,
conquered.

But will this feeling linger,
or will it sink with the new dawn,
shattered by a storm of emotions,
leaving behind only fragments of joy?

Soon, it will all be a distant memory,
and the eyes that praised me
will look away.

Why would I feel that way? Perhaps,
they told me to play their game,
a game they invented,
a game they control.

Perhaps winning is my escape,
but I am more than a player,
more than a prize.

I exist to experience the cosmos—
the seen and the unseen,
the known and the unknown.

Each day brings a new battle,
but with it, the chance
to give love,
to be love,
and to find myself in the vastness of the cosmos.

12. Can't stop the Sun

Come find me in my acts-
of love, kindness and strength.

Don't reduce me to the perceptions,
or compare me,
you think you can summarize me,
with a few words, carelessly tossed?

When you get to me,
speak to the corner of heart,
that treasures the spirit of life,
the moments with you,
holds the pain of failures past
and bold decisions to fight storms.

Speak to the silence in there-
the knowing of the people, the reality,
measuring your worth when all you did was to care.

Growing up a in sea of expectation,
bundling on my shoulders--
no matter how much i swim,
everything seems to be afar.

A loser for not reaching the horizon,
a believer for finding one.

You were meant to free me,
swim with me,
but here you lay your eyes--
a critic like others,
illusions of you being different,
vanished, destroyed,
and burnt,
now the ashes spread up with wind,
reminding me the importance of win,
still i keep swimming, dreaming,
searching for the life's meaning
with or without you.

13. And the Sun sets

Oh time, I beg and beg,
walk slowly when she holds my hand,
when I chase sunsets, sing songs,
and laugh with dear friends.

Oh time, I beg and beg,
race ahead when I am broken,
when tears fill my eyes,
and loneliness fills the night.

Oh time, I beg and beg,
take me back to childhood days—
dancing in the rain, racing through streets,
living so loudly
that escape never crossed my mind.

Oh time, I beg and beg,
pause for a while
when the soul is happy and kind,
when the sun shines bright,
and the moon hangs above the ocean,
casting its silver light.
Pause when I hike mountains and trails.

Oh time, grant me the power
to move back and forth,
to know the storms and the rain,
the blissful days yet to come.
But I wonder—would that steal away
the art, the poems, the songs?
Would we still ache to express,
or would nothing be lost?

14. Evenings: Let go of what is behind

Strange world of love—

if love is unreturned, you write of your longings;
if found and lost, you write of that dream;
if found and kept, you no longer write—
you simply speak,
for you have become poetry itself.

You shine in the books I write,
though I try to keep you away.
Let the words reach for the sun, the moon, and time,
yet in the end, they always return—
back to you.

My diary is filled with you—
the days you cared for me,
written in detail: the silence of sitting with you,
the loudness of laughing with you.

There are only so many words I can write,
for my art is not so sublime.
It could never do justice to your eyes,

so if I ever stop writing about you,
know it's the failure of my art,
not of my love for you.

Take all the space you need in my books,
but allow me to write of things that are not about you.
Let me go, for I am no longer close to you,
for the poems no longer grow stronger with you.

Now I write, and I feel free.
Now you no longer appear in my dreams.
Now I've let go of hoping for your return—
the pages of that diary now burned.

15. The Nights and Lost stars

I saw a book,
I lifted it up.
"Why are you crying?" I asked,
to which the book replied:

"I can no longer say I am gifted,
I was made that way.
I have tried to be everything—
been the topics, the words you could relate to.
I don't feel like I have it in me anymore.
The hope of reaching you is lost.

I belong in the grave now,
in the graveyard of forgotten art.
I will not be the words you read to a lover,
I will not be the lines you turn to when you suffer.
No eyes will linger on me at supper,
no mug of coffee will sit beside me now.
In happiness, I will not be remembered.

Friends of mine have been here for ages,
still, the world talks about them.

They carry magic in their veins,
I carry mortal blood.
I was just born,
but every star is not meant to live forever.
Every star is not the sun.
Some die, lost in the Milky Way or across galaxies.

The one who wrote me said,
'You are not my heart,
you are my soul.'

He lied, oh, take me to
where I belong."

16. Back in time, Back in days

Sometimes I go back to a place,
but it doesn't feel the same—
I can't recapture the way it used to be.

Instead, I long to return
to a place at a particular time:
my hometown.

If I am a vast tree,
with fruits of success, regrets,
friends, relationships, adventures, and lessons
hanging from my branches,
my roots remain in that town.

Be it evenings playing cricket,
laughing with cousins, lost in conversations
that made no sense,
or paper boats on rainy days,
I felt special, every day, every season.
I was fully present,
never thinking beyond the moment,
unaware of time slipping through my fingers.

Those were the happiest days of my life,
and I didn't even realize it.

Now, the town has changed.
For me, everything lives in memories.

But one thing remains:
the power of revival.
When I am stressed,
worried about the future,
lost in the crowd,
and tired of the present,
I go back to that town.

It reminds me of how far I've come.
Even if you cut down the whole tree,
strip away everything,
there will still be a roof
where you are welcomed,
a place that inspires you,
to water your roots again,
and help you grow again.

"You can conquer the world,
be anywhere in the world,
but when you bleed,
it's always that soil and air you will ever need."

17. Tomorrow

I have lost a thousand times,
broken at times,
watched the sun always setting,
my dreams burning.

I thought of giving up,
believing that climbing up
and reaching the top
was just an illusion—
perhaps a world of delusion.

At the bottom of the rock,
I saw a hawk,
flying around the peak,
mocking,
saying:

"You live in a room
with a door closed.
The universe can only knock
from the outside.
You must open it
from within."

Now I open the door,
step out,
and feel the light.
Everything won't change in an instant,
but I will be a step closer to change—
one that will wash away the sand
of fear and resistance from my eyes,
so I can see clearly, fearlessly.

For now, I will walk.

18. Magical Mornings

I turn back,
signs before my eyes,
telling me what I lack.
My body aches to escape,
to run away under a different sky.

This sky is dark and cloudy,
with lightning strikes.
My belief in myself hides.
For how long can I lie,
pretending to be fine?

The words are so loud,
even on a mountain of doubts,
I hear them.

Maybe I can turn them to my blind side,
but healing is not about running away
or fighting back.

It's about creating a shield,
so your mind won't yield,
your heart won't bleed.

It's about reinventing,
rediscovering,
beginning again
at your own pace,
letting go of what you don't need.

The weather will change.
You'll stand at the shore,
holding a surfboard,
fearlessly riding waves
meant to take you down,
crush your crown.

Looking back, you'll laugh
with your friends,
wondering why you wished
for a magical wand.
The magic you desired for so long
was inside you all along.

19. Photographs: Glimpses of yesterday

I have photographs,
of you and me.
See in them—
memories breathe,
smiles sing.

I keep them close,
writing on the back—
funny details, something abstract:

On the mountain highs,
a valley named Spiti,
we rode a motorcycle,
climbing to 11,980 feet of life.
"On the top,
oxygen finite,
but here we breathe as if we are infinite."

On the beaches of Goa,
we walked, felt all the shades—
sunshine, sunsets—
all with my beloved friends.

"Noises, worries, heaviness—all converged
into peace, love, and warmth.
The feeling of being reborn,
a moment forever worn."

Snorkeling in the shallow waters of Bali,
seeing the life below, mesmerized completely.
"Transported to a different world—
colors brighter, sounds lighter,
new to the eyes, a magical paradise.
A moment transcending the shackles of time."

From mountains to shores,
cities across,
photographs of you and me—
they speak it all.

20. Forget what happened yesterday

When I say, "Hey, what's up,"
I mean to say:
talk to me about everything you did today,
ask how I am—

for I hide a thousand different emotions
behind these words;
for I hide the courage it took to text you,
knowing you might not reply for days.

I would gift you flowers—
please don't mind—
don't over calculate the circumstances,
the intentions behind,
It is just my love for you,
spilling out of me,
uncontainable.

Don't judge me when I say
you look so beautiful today—
it is the truth of the universe,
hidden in my heart,

that slipped out,
unbidden.

That is me simply reaching out to you,
holding nothing back.

Sorry if you get confused;
sometimes I will take a step
to act on what my heart says.
Forgive me; forget it,
like a night's dream.

For it is my mistake
to have presented it in a dramatic way.
For now, I will hold down and not let a thought slip out.

Even on drunk nights,
even when I stand lost in my own land,
I will carry this love quietly,
like a secret the moon whispers to the sea.

21. The End

Hello, you—
this is the last poem I'll write for you.
It may not sound like one,
but it is the celebration of writing multiple ones.

I am at the finish line now,
no longer a prisoner of dreams.
My hopeful, optimistic self stole a win,
even if no copies of it are sold,
I did something bold.

If I can somehow be here,
then why don't you dare to dream,
to act, and leave the past behind?

For the book has ended now,
but the journey goes on.
I don't know what this will become,
but I had to give it all.

I might not write again,
but I had to give it a go.
For whatever it's worth,

you'll never know what's beyond that door
until you start knocking,
and tell destiny—
"Open it up for me."

22. Thoughts turned into poem 1

If I felt alive with you,
on the stormy days,
I would sit in silence with you.

when your heart beat for the last time.

Beside your grave, I would walk,
and sing a hymn
for how a part of me was born
in the light of your existence,
and how it died with you.

In the graveyard, buried are not just those who die,
but also the shards of life
they carry away from the beings
well and still alive.

23. Thoughts turned into poem 2

Have we grown apart?
Once, we were swimming,
side by side,
singing the same songs,
but these waves
took us to different shores.

Now, I can see you
on another end,
standing on unfamiliar sand,
exploring a different land.

Somedays, we might take a boat,
rowing through the waves,
to a shared shore,
with a bottle of wine,
wishing to find shores,
of a thousand different kinds,
and each other,
in a thousand different times.

24. Thought turned into poem 3

I fell into the darkest corner of a cave,
nightmares visible in haze,
no place for light.
What am I supposed to chase?
What will it take from me
to escape this place, this time?

I don't have the strength left in me
to fight the battles of change.
For now, I just want to lie in hope,
to see a shard of the sun walk to me,
to pull me out.

I have burned too much,
with fires ignited by the world.
I do not belong here,
yet I suffer, endure,
this world looks down on me.

For I always find my way back to that cave,
and never to the mountain's peak,
built of people and the money that binds them.

25. Thoughts turned into poem 4

I wonder how a poem comes to life.
Maybe it was on a day
a heart was broken, or
someone died, or
failure struck,
someone felt lost, or
overflowing with joy,
loved in return,
traveled to a distant place,
returned home,
met a long-lost friend,
or drifted away from them.

Maybe it was when
someone believed,
felt the universe's magic,
floated in oceans of imagination,
crossed an item off their bucket list,
remembered days long gone,
paused to observe,
won a battle,
or simply lived a day in life.

"The life you live,
is a poetry that breathes"